Patterns for Vintage Doilies

Crochet Doily Patterns (Beginner to Advanced)

Copyright © 2024

DEDICATION

Contents

Dawnglow

Materials needed-

1 ball of size 10 crochet thread

1.75 mm hook

Special stitches-

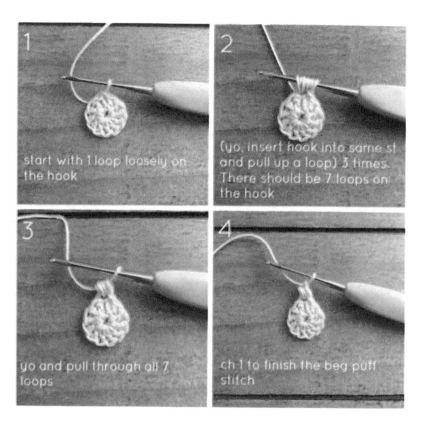

beg puff stitch- with 1 loop loosely on the hook, (yo, insert hook into same st and pull up a loop) 3 times, yo and pull through all 7 loops on hook, ch 1

Step 1- yo, insert hook into space indicated and pull up a loop, (yo, insert hook into same st and pull up a loop) twice. There should be 7 loops on the hook.

Step 2- yo and pull through 6 loops on hook. There should be 2 loops remaining on the hook.

Step 3- yo and pull throug the last 2 loops to complete the puff stitch.

puff stitch- yo, insert hook into st indicated and pull up a loop, (yo, insert hook into same st and pull up a loop) twice (there should be 7 loops), yo and pull through 6 loops on hook, yo and pull through last 2 loops on hook

beg cluster- ch 2, dc in space indicated

cluster- keeping last loop of each dc on hook, 2 dc in st or space indicated, yo and draw through all 3 loops on hook

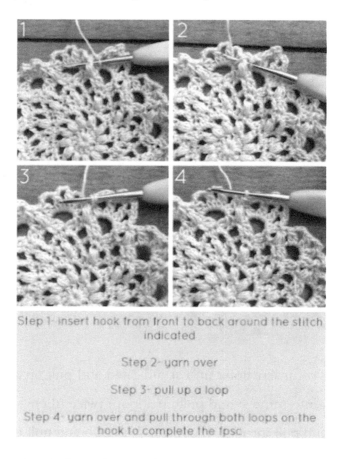

Step 1- insert hook from front to back around the stitch indicated

Step 2- yarn over

Step 3- pull up a loop

Step 4- yarn over and pull through both loops on the hook to complete the fpsc

fpsc- insert hook from front to back around st indicated, yo and pull up a loop, yo and pull through both loops on hook

picot- ch 3, sl st in last sc

beg 2-dc decrease- ch 2, dc in next dc

2-dc decrease- keeping last loop of each dc on hook, dc in next 2 dc, yo and draw through all 3 loops on hook

large picot- ch 3, sl st in 3rd ch from hook, ch 1

Instructions-

On rounds 3 to 18 repeat from [to] until you reach the end of the round and make a sl st where indicated.

ch 4, sl st in fourth ch from hook to make a ring

Rnd 1- ch 3 (counts as first dc), 11 dc in ring, sl st in third ch of first dc (12 dc)

Rnd 2- beg puff stitch in same st, ch 2, (puff stitch in next dc, ch 2) around, sl st in first ch of beg puff stitch (12 puff stitches, 12 spaces)

Rnd 3- ch 1, sc in same st, (dc, ch 3, dc) in next space, [sc in next puff st, (dc, ch 3, dc) in next space] around, sl st in first dc

Rnd 4- beg puff stitch in same st, ch 3, sc in next space, ch 3, [puff stitch in next sc, ch 3, sc in next space, ch 3] around, sl st in first ch of beg puff stitch

Rnd 5- ch 1, sc in same st, sc in next space, ch 5, sc in next space, [sc in next puff st, sc in next space, ch 5, sc in next space] around, sl st in first sc

Rnd 6- (beg cluster, ch 5, cluster) in same st, sc in next space, [sk next sc, (cluster, ch 5, cluster) in next sc, sc in next space] around, sl st in first cluster

Rnd 7- sl st in next space, beg cluster, (ch 3, cluster)3 times in same space, puff stitch in next sc, [cluster in next space, (ch 3, cluster) 3 times in same space, puff stitch in next sc] around, sl st in first cluster

Rnd 8- sl st in next space, ch 1, sc in same space, ch 3, (sc, ch 3) twice in next space, sc in next space, fpsc around next puff stitch, picot, [sc in next space, ch 3, (sc, ch 3) twice in next space, sc in next space, fpsc around next puff stitch, picot] around, sl st in first sc

Rnd 9- sl st in next space, ch 1, sc in same space, 7 dc in next space, sc in next space, ch 5, [sc in next space, 7 dc in next space, sc in next space, ch 5] around, sl st in first sc

Rnd 10- sl st in next dc, ch 3 (counts as first dc, now and throughout), sc in next dc, (ch 3, sc in next dc) 4 times, dc in next dc, ch 2, sc in next space, ch 2, [dc in next dc, sc in next dc, (ch 3, sc in next dc) 4 times, dc in next dc, ch 2, sc in next space, ch 2] around, sl st in third ch of first dc

Rnd 11- ch 3, sc in next space, (ch 3, sc in next space) 3 times, dc in next dc, ch 3, [dc in next dc, sc in next space, (ch 3, sc in next space) 3 times, dc in next dc, ch 3] around, sl st in third ch of first dc

Rnd 12- ch 3, sc in next space, (ch 3, sc in next space) twice, dc in next dc, ch 3, puff stitch in center ch of next space, ch 3, [dc in next dc, sc in next space, (ch 3, sc in next space) twice, dc in next dc, ch 3, puff stitch in center ch of next space, ch 3] around, sl st in third ch of first dc

Rnd 13- (ch 3, sc in next space) twice, dc in next dc, ch 5, sc in next space, fpsc around next puff stitch, picot, sc in next space, ch 5, [dc in next dc, sc in next space, ch 3, sc in next space, dc in next dc, ch 5, sc in next space, fpsc around next puff stitch, picot, sc in next space, ch 5] around, sl st in third ch of first dc

Rnd 14- ch 3, sc in next space, dc in next dc, ch 5, sc in next space, ch 7, sc in next space, ch 5, [dc in next dc, sc in next space, dc in next dc, ch 5, sc in next space, ch 7, sc in next space, ch 5] around, sl st in third ch of first dc

Rnd 15- beg 2-dc decrease, ch 5, sc in next space, 11 dc in next space, sc in next space, ch 5, [2-dc decrease, ch 5, sc in next space, 11 dc in next space, sc in next space, ch 5] around, sl st in first 2-dc decrease

Rnd 16- sl st in next 3 ch, ch 1, sc in same space, dc in next dc, (ch 1, dc in next dc) 10 times, sc in next space, ch 5, [sc in next space, dc in next dc, (ch 1, dc in next dc) 10 times, sc in next space, ch 5] around, sl st in first sc

Rnd 17- sl st in next dc, ch 5 (counts as first dc and ch 2), dc in next dc, (ch 2, dc in next dc) 9 times, sc in next space, [dc in next dc, (ch 2, dc in next dc) 10 times, sc in next space] around, sl st in third ch of first dc

Rnd 18- ch 1, sc in same st, ch 2, (sc in next dc, large picot, sc in next dc, ch 2) twice, sc in next space, large picot, sc in next space, ch 2, (sc in next dc, large picot, sc in next dc, ch 2) twice, sc in next dc, sk next sc, [sc in next dc, ch 2, (sc in next dc, large picot, sc in next dc, ch 2) twice, sc in next space, large picot, sc in next space, ch 2, (sc in next dc, large picot, sc in next dc, ch 2) twice, sc in next dc, sk next sc] around, sl st in first sc, fasten off and weave in ends

Shamrock Soiree

This pattern has 23 rounds and measures about 10 1/2" in diameter.

Pattern is written using U.S. Terminology.

Materials

size 10 thread in 2 colors-

Patterns for Vintage Doilies

color 1- 125-150 yards

color 2- 5-10 yards

1.75 mm hook

yarn needle

scissors

Stitch Abbreviations

beg- beginning

BPdc- back post double crochet

ch(s)- chains

dc- double crochet

FPdc- front post double crochet

FPsc- front post single crochet

hdc- half double crochet

LS- left side

RS- right side

sc- single crochet

sc-BLO- single crochet back loop only

st(s)- stitch(es)

yo- yarn over

Special Stitches

beg 4-dc cluster- (uses same ch-3 space and next ch-3 space), ch 2, keeping last loop of each dc on hook, dc in same space, 2 dc in next ch-3 space, yo and draw through all 4 loops on hook.

4-dc cluster- (uses same ch-3 space and next ch-3 space), keeping last loop of each dc on hook, 2 dc in same ch-3 space, 2 dc in next ch-3 space, yo and draw through all 5 loops on hook.

2-dc decrease- keeping last loop of each dc on hook, dc in each of the next 2 sts indicated, yo and draw through all 3 loops on hook.

3-dc decrease- keeping last loop of each dc on hook, dc in each of the next 3 sts indicated, yo and draw through all 4 loops on hook.

2-FPsc decrease- insert hook from front to back around the post of the first st indicated, yo and pull up a loop, insert hook from front to back around the post of the next st indicated, yo and pull up a loop, yo and draw through all 3 loops on hook.

3-dc popcorn- ch 3 (counts as first dc), dc twice in st indicated, drop loop from hook, insert hook in the third ch of first dc, pick up the dropped loop and pull through.

2-FPdc decrease- keeping last loop of each FPdc on hook, FPdc around the post of each of the next 2 sts indicated, yo and draw through all 3 loops on hook.

2-FPdc cluster- keeping last loop of each FPdc on hook, FPdc twice around the post of the st indicated, yo and draw through all 3 loops on hook.

beg 3-dc cluster- ch 2, keeping last loop of each dc on hook, 2 dc in the same ch-3 space indicated, yo and draw through all 3 loops on hook.

3-dc cluster- keeping last loop of each dc on hook, 3 dc in the ch-3 space indicated, yo and draw through all 4 loops on hook.

3-FPdc decrease(RS)- keeping last loop of each FPdc on hook, FPdc twice around next FPdc, FPdc around next FPdc, yo and draw through all 4 loops on hook.

3-FPdc decrease(LS)- keeping last loop of each FPdc on hook, FPdc around next FPdc, FPdc twice around next FPdc, yo and draw through all 4 loops on hook.

picot- ch 3, slip st in third ch from hook.

large picot- ch 5, slip st in fifth ch from hook.

Notes

[ ] - work enclosed instructions the amount of times indicated, or work enclosed instructions in the stitch or space indicated.

- repeat the following instructions the amount of times indicated.

( ) - Enclose additional information.

Text highlighted in this color means that there are photos and additional information below.

Instructions

ch 4, slip st in first ch to make a ring.

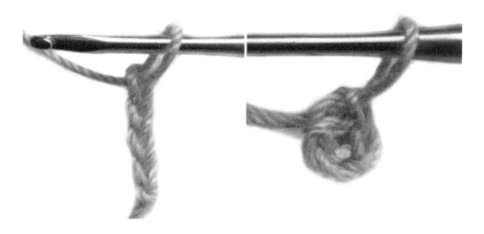

Round 1

ch 3 (counts as first dc), 15 dc in ring, slip st to third ch of first dc.

(16 dc)

Round 2

ch 1, sc in same st, [ch 3, skip next dc, sc in next dc] 7 times, ch 1, hdc in first sc to make last ch-3 space.

(8 sc, 8 ch-3 spaces)

Round 3

beg 4-dc cluster using same ch-3 space and next ch-3 space, [ch 5, 4-dc cluster using same ch-3 space and next ch-3 space] around, ch 2, dc in beg 4-dc cluster to make last ch-5 space.

(8 4-dc clusters, 8 ch-5 spaces)

Round 3- Beg 4-dc cluster

1- ch 2.

2- yo and insert hook into the same ch-3 space and pull up a loop, yo and draw through 2 loops on hook. (2 loops on hook)

3- yo and insert hook into the next ch-3 space, yo and pull up a loop, yo and draw through 2 loops on hook. (3 loops on hook)

4- yo and insert hook into the same ch-3 space, yo and pull up a loop, yo and draw through 2 loops on hook. (4 loops on hook)

5- yo and draw through all 4 loops on hook to complete the beg 4-dc cluster.

Round 3- 4-dc cluster

1- You'll be working in the same ch-3 space and next ch-3 space, both circled in the first photo.

2- [yo and insert hook into the same ch-3 space, yo and pull up a loop, yo and draw through 2 loops on hook] twice. (3 loops on hook)

3- [yo and insert hook into the next ch-3 space, yo and pull up a loop, yo and draw through 2 loops on hook] twice. (5 loops on hook).

4- yo and draw through all 5 loops on hook to complete the 4-dc cluster.

Round 4

ch 1, 3 sc in same space, ch 3, slip st in third ch from hook (picot made), [3 sc, ch 3] twice in next ch-5 space, slip st in third ch from hook (picot made), repeat from around, 3 sc in same ch-5 space as first sc, ch 1, hdc in first sc to make last ch-3 space.

(48 sc, 8 ch-3 spaces)

Round 5

ch 8 (counts as first dc and ch-5 space), skip next 6 sc, [dc, ch 3, dc] in next ch-3 space, ch 5, skip next 6 sc, repeat from around, dc in same ch-3 space as first dc, ch 3, slip st to third ch of first dc.

(16 dc, 8 ch-3 spaces, 8 ch-5 spaces)

Round 6

ch 3 (counts as first dc), dc in same st, ch 3, sc in next ch-5 space, ch 3, 2 dc in next dc, ch 3, skip next ch-3 space, [2 dc in next dc, ch 3, sc in next ch-5 space, ch 3, 2 dc in next dc, ch 3, skip next ch-3 space] around, slip st to third ch of first dc.

(32 dc, 24 ch-3 spaces, 8 sc)

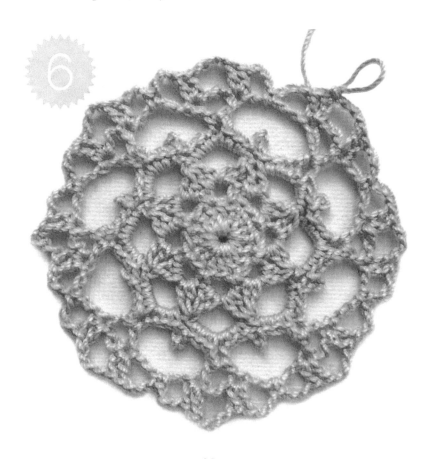

Round 7

ch 3 (counts as first dc), 2 dc in next dc, sc in next ch-3 space, ch 3, sc in next ch-3 space, 2 dc in next dc, dc in next dc, ch 5, dc in next dc, 2 dc in next dc, sc in next ch-3 space, ch 3, sc in next ch-3 space, 2 dc in next dc, dc in next dc, ch 5, repeat from around, slip st to third ch of first dc.

(48 dc, 8 ch-5 spaces, 16 sc, 8 ch-3 spaces)

Round 8

ch 2, dc in next dc (first 2-dc decrease made), 2 dc in next dc, sc in next ch-3 space, 2 dc in next dc, 2-dc decrease in next 2 dc, ch 3, [dc, ch 3] twice in center ch of next ch-5 space, 2-dc decrease in next 2 dc, 2 dc in next dc, sc in next ch-3 space, 2 dc in next dc, 2-dc decrease in next 2 dc, ch 3,[dc, ch 3] twice in center ch of next ch-5 space, repeat from around, slip st to top of first 2-dc decrease.

(48 dc, 16 2-dc decreases, 24 ch-3 spaces)

Round 8- 2-dc decrease in next 2 dc

1- yo and insert hook into the first dc indicated, yo and pull up a loop, yo and draw through 2 loops on hook. (2 loops on hook)

2- yo and insert hook into the second dc indicated, yo and pull up a loop, yo and draw through 2 loops on hook. (3 loops on hook)

3- yo and draw through all 3 loops on hook to complete the 2-dc decrease.

Round 9

ch 2, dc in next dc (first 2-dc decrease made), dc in each of next 3 sts, 2-dc decrease in next 2 sts, ch 3, skip next ch-3 space, 9 dc in next ch-3 space, ch 3, skip next ch-3 space, [2-dc decrease in next 2 sts, dc in each of next 3 sts, 2-dc decrease in next 2 sts, ch 3, skip next ch-3 space, 9 dc in next ch-3 space, ch 3, skip next ch-3 space] around, slip st to top of first 2-dc decrease.

(96 dc, 16 2-dc decreases, 16 ch-3 spaces)

Round 10

ch 2, dc in next dc (first 2-dc decrease made), dc in next dc, 2-dc decrease in next 2 sts, ch 3, dc in next dc, BPdc around next dc, BPdc twice around next dc, sc in each of next 3 dc, BPdc twice around next dc, BPdc around next dc, dc in next dc, ch 3, skip next ch-3 space, 2-dc decrease in next 2 sts, dc in next dc, 2-dc decrease in next 2 sts, ch 3, dc in next dc, BPdc around next dc, BPdc twice around next dc, sc in each of next 3 dc, BPdc twice around next dc, BPdc around next dc, dc in next dc, ch 3, skip next ch-3 space, repeat from around, slip st to top of first 2- dc decrease.

(16 2-dc decreases, 24 dc, 16 ch-3 spaces, 48 BPdc, 24 sc)

Round 10- How to make a BPdc

1- yo.

2 and 3- insert hook from back to front around the post of the next dc indicated.

4- yo and pull up a loop.

5- [yo and draw through 2 loops on hook] twice to complete the BPdc.

Round 11

ch 2, 2-dc decrease in next 2 sts (counts as first 3-dc decrease), ch 3, FPdc twice around next dc, [sc in next BPdc, ch 1] 3 times, sc in each of next 3 sc, [ch 1, sc in next BPdc] 3 times, FPdc twice around next dc (optional- work second FPdc behind the first FPdc), ch 3, skip next ch-3 space, 3-dc decrease in next 3 sts, ch 3, FPdc twice around next dc, [sc in next BPdc, ch 1] 3 times, sc in each of next 3 sc, [ch 1, sc in next BPdc] 3 times, FPdc twice around next dc (optional- work second FPdc behind the first FPdc), ch 3, skip next ch-3 space, repeat from around, slip st to top of first 3-dc decrease.

(16 3-dc decreases, 16 ch-3 spaces, 32 FPdc, 72 sc, 48 ch-1 spaces)

Round 11- How to make a FPdc

1- yo.

2- insert hook from front to back around the post of the st indicated.

3 and 4- yo and pull up a loop, [yo and draw through 2 loops on hook] twice to complete the the FPdc.

Round 11- (optional) work second FPdc behind the first FPdc

1- After making the first FPdc, move it forward slightly so you can work behind it.

2- yo and insert hook from front to back around the same st.

3- yo and pull up a loop, [yo and draw through 2 loops on hook] twice.

Round 12

ch 6 (counts as first dc and ch-3 space), 2-FPsc decrease around next

2 FPdc, 3-dc popcorn in last 2-FPsc decrease made, [sc in next ch-1 space, ch 1] 3 times, skip next sc, sc in next sc, [ch 1, sc in next ch-1 space] 3 times, 3-dc popcorn in last sc made, 2-FPsc decrease around next 2 FPdc, ch 3, dc in next 3-dc decrease, ch 3, 2-FPsc decrease around next 2 FPdc, 3-dc popcorn in last 2-FPsc decrease made, [sc in next ch-1 space, ch 1] 3 times, skip next sc, sc in next sc, [ch 1, sc in next ch-1 space] 3 times, 3-dc popcorn in last sc made, 2-FPsc decrease around next 2 FPdc, ch 3, repeat from around, slip st to third ch of first dc.

Mark 3rd sc made for st placement on Round 14.

(8 dc, 16 ch-3 spaces, 16 2-FPsc decreases, 16 3-dc popcorns, 56 sc, 48 ch-1 spaces)

Round 12- 2-FPsc decrease

1- you will be working around the posts of the 2 FPdcs circled in the first photo.

2- insert hook from front to back around the post of the first FPdc indicated.

3- yo and pull up a loop.

4- insert hook from front to back around the post of the second FPdc indicated, yo and pull up a loop.

5- yo and draw through all 3 loops on hook.

Round 12- 3-dc popcorn

1- ch 3.

2- 2 dc in the last 2-FPsc decrease made.

3- drop loop from the hook and insert it into the third ch of the first dc made.

4- pick up the dropped loop.

5- pull the loop through to complete the 3-dc popcorn.

Round 13

ch 6 (counts as first dc and ch-3 space), dc in same st, ch 3, skip next 2-FPsc decrease and next 3-dc popcorn, 2 dc in next sc, dc in next ch-1 space, hdc in next sc, sc in next ch-1 space, [ch 1, sc in next ch-1 space] 3 times, hdc in next sc, dc in next ch-1 space, 2 dc in next sc (same st that the 3-dc popcorn was made in), ch 3, skip next 3-dc popcorn and next 2-FPsc decrease, [dc, ch 3] twice in next dc, skip next 2-FPsc decrease and next 3-dc popcorn, 2 dc in next sc, dc in next ch-1 space, hdc in next sc, sc in next ch-1 space, [ch 1, sc in next ch-1 space] 3 times, hdc in next sc, dc in next ch-1 space, 2 dc in next sc (same st that the 3-dc popcorn was made in), ch 3, skip next 3-dc popcorn and next 2-FPsc decrease, repeat from around, slip st to third ch of first dc.

(64 dc, 24 ch-3 spaces, 16 hdc, 32 sc, 24 ch-1 spaces)

Round 14

ch 5 (counts as first dc and ch-2 space), 2 dc in next ch-3 space, ch 2, dc in next dc, ch 3, 2-FPdc decrease around next 2 dc, 3-dc popcorn in last 2-FPdc decrease made, 2-FPdc cluster around marked sc on Round 12, skip next 3 sts on Round 13, sc in next ch-1 space on Round 13, [ch 1, sc in next sc, ch 1, sc in next ch-1 space] twice, skip next sc on Round 12, 2-FPdc cluster around next sc on Round 12, 3-dc popcorn in last 2-FPdc cluster made, skip next 3 sts on Round 13, 2-FPdc decrease around next 2 dc on Round 13, ch 3,   dc in next dc, ch 2, 2 dc in next ch-3 space, ch 2, dc in next dc, ch 3, 2-FPdc decrease around next 2 dc, 3-dc popcorn in last 2-FPdc decrease made, 2-FPdc cluster around third sc on Round 12 of the shamrock, skip next 3 sts on Round 13, sc in next ch-1 space on Round 13, [ch 1, sc in next sc, ch 1, sc in next ch-1 space] twice, skip next sc on Round 12, 2-FPdc cluster around next sc on Round 12, 3-dc popcorn in last 2-FPdc cluster made, skip next 3 sts on Round 13, 2-FPdc decrease around next 2 dc on Round 13, ch 3, repeat from   around, slip st to third ch of first dc.

Mark 3rd sc made for st placement on Round 17.

(32 dc, 16 ch-2 spaces, 16 ch-3 spaces, 16 2-FPdc decreases, 16 3-dc popcorns,40 sc, 16 2-FPdc clusters, 32 ch-1 spaces)

Round 14- 2-FPdc cluster around marked sc on Round 12

1- you will be working around the post of the sc circled in the first photo.

2- yo and insert hook from front to back around the post of the sc indicated.

3- yo and pull up a loop.

4- yo and draw through 2 loops on hook.

5- Repeat steps 2-4 once more. (3 loops left on the hook).

6- yo and draw through all 3 loops on hook to complete the 2-FPdc cluster.

Round 14- 2-FPdc cluster around next sc on Round 12

Skip the next sc on Round 12. Working around the sc circled in the photo below, follow the same instructions as the last 2-FPdc cluster made.

Round 15

ch 6 (counts as first dc and ch-3 space), sc in next ch-2 space, ch 2, FPdc around next 2 dc together as 1 st, ch 2, sc in next ch-2 space, ch 3, dc in next dc, ch 3, skip next 2-FPdc decrease and next 3-dc popcorn, dc twice in next 2-FPdc cluster, sc in next ch-1 space, [ch 1, sc in next ch-1 space] 3 times, dc twice in next 2-FPdc cluster (same st that the 3-dc popcorn is in), ch 3, skip next 3-dc popcorn and next 2-FPdc decrease,   dc in next dc, ch 3, sc in next ch-2 space, ch 2, FPdc around next 2 dc together as 1 st, ch 2, sc in next ch-2 space, ch 3, dc in next dc, ch 3, skip next 2-FPdc decrease and next 3-dc popcorn, dc twice in next 2-FPdc cluster, sc in next ch-1 space, [ch 1, sc in next ch-1 space] 3 times, dc twice in next 2-FPdc cluster (same st that the 3-dc popcorn is in), ch 3, skip next 3-dc popcorn and next 2-FPdc decrease, repeat from   around, slip st to third ch of first dc.

(48 dc, 32 ch-3 spaces, 48 sc, 16 ch-2 spaces, 8 FPdc, 24 ch-1 spaces)

Round 16

ch 3 (counts as first dc), dc in same st, ch 3, 2-dc cluster in next sc, [dc, hdc] in next ch-2 space, sc in next FPdc, [hdc, dc] in next ch-2 space, 2-dc cluster in next sc, ch 3, dc twice in next dc, ch 3, FPdc around each of next 2 dc, sc in next ch-1 space (mark this sc for st placement on Round 18), [ch 1, sc in next ch-1 space] twice, FPdc around each of next 2 dc, ch 3,   dc twice in next dc, ch 3, 2-dc cluster in next sc, [dc, hdc] in next ch-2 space, sc in next FPdc, [hdc, dc] in next ch-2 space, 2-dc cluster in next sc, ch 3, dc twice in next dc, ch 3, FPdc around each of next 2 dc, sc in next ch-1 space, [ch 1, sc in next ch-1 space] twice, FPdc around each of next 2 dc, ch 3, repeat from around, slip st to third ch of first dc.

(48 dc, 32 ch-3 spaces, 16 2-dc clusters, 16 hdc, 32 sc, 32 FPdc, 16 ch-1 spaces)

Round 17

ch 3 (counts as first dc), dc in same st, dc twice in next dc, ch 3, 2-FPdc cluster around next 2-dc cluster, FPdc around each of next 5 sts, 2-FPdc cluster around next 2-dc cluster, ch 3, dc twice in each of next 2 dc, ch 3, 2-FPdc decrease around next 2 FPdc, 3-dc popcorn in last 2-FPdc decrease made, sc in the marked sc on Round 14, 3-dc popcorn in last sc made, 2-FPdc decrease around next 2 FPdc on Round 16, ch 3, dc twice in each of next 2 dc, ch 3, 2-FPdc cluster around next 2-dc cluster, FPdc around each of next 5 sts, 2-FPdc cluster around next 2-dc cluster, ch 3, dc twice in each of next 2 dc, ch 3, 2-FPdc decrease around next 2 FPdc, 3-dc popcorn in last 2-FPdc decrease made, sc in the 3rd sc (center sc on the shamrock) on Round 14, 3-dc popcorn in last sc made, 2-FPdc decrease around next 2 FPdc on Round 16, ch 3, repeat from around, slip st to third ch of first dc.

(64 dc, 32 ch-3 spaces, 16 2-FPdc clusters, 40 FPdc, 16 2-FPdc decreases, 16 3-dc popcorns, 8 sc)

Round 17- sc in the marked sc on Round 14

1- you'll be working around the post of the sc circled in the first photo.

2- insert hook from front to back around the post of the sc indicated.

3- yo and pull up a loop, yo and draw through 2 loops on hook to complete the sc.

Round 18

ch 4 (counts as first dc and ch-1 space), dc in next dc, [ch 1, dc in next dc] twice, ch 3, skip next 2-FPdc cluster and next FPdc, FPdc twice around next FPdc, FPdc around next FPdc, FPdc twice around next FPdc (optional- work second FPdc behind the last FPdc made), ch 3, skip next FPdc and next 2-FPdc cluster, dc in next dc, [ch 1, dc in next dc] 3 times, ch 3, working behind the sts made on Round 17- sc in the marked sc on Round 16, ch 3, [sc in the next sc on Round 16, ch 3] twice,   dc in next dc on Round 17, [ch 1, dc in next dc] twice, ch 3, skip next 2-FPdc cluster and next FPdc, FPdc twice around next FPdc, FPdc around next FPdc, FPdc twice around next FPdc (optional- work second FPdc behind the last FPdc made), ch 3, skip next FPdc and next 2-FPdc cluster, dc in next dc, [ch 1, dc in next dc] 3 times, ch 3, working behind the sts made on Round 17- sc in the first sc of the next shamrock on Round 16, ch 3, [sc in the next sc on Round 16, ch 3] twice, repeat from around, slip st to third ch of first dc.

(64 dc, 48 ch-1 spaces, 48 ch-3 spaces, 40 FPdc, 24 sc)

Round 18- sc in the marked sc on Round 16

1- you'll be working the sc circled in the first photo and behind the sts on Round 17.

2- sc in the sc indicated.

3-d ch 3, [sc in the next sc on Round 15, ch 3] twice.

Round 19

slip st in next ch-1 space, beg 3-dc cluster in same space, ch 3, [3-dc cluster in next ch-1 space, ch 3] twice, sc in next ch-3 space, ch 3, 3-FPdc decrease(RS) around next 2 FPdc, ch 1, FPsc around next FPdc, ch 1, 3-FPdc decrease(LS) around next 2 FPdc, ch 3, sc in next ch-3 space, ch 3, [3-dc cluster in next ch-1 space, ch 3] 3 times, skip next ch-3 space, [sc in next ch-3 space, ch 3] twice, skip next ch-3 space, 3-dc cluster in next ch-1 space, ch 3, [3-dc cluster in next ch-1 space, ch 3] twice, sc in next ch-3 space, ch 3, 3-FPdc decrease(RS) around next 2 FPdc, ch 1, FPsc around next FPdc, ch 1, 3-FPdc decrease(LS) around next 2 FPdc, ch 3, sc in next ch-3 space, ch 3, [3-dc cluster in next ch-1 space, ch 3] 3 times, skip next ch-3 space, [sc in next ch-3 space, ch 3] twice, skip next ch-3 space, repeat from   around, slip st to top of first 3-dc cluster.

(48 3-dc clusters, 88 ch-3 spaces, 32 sc, 16 3-FPdc decreases, 16 ch-1 spaces, 8 FPsc)

Round 19- beg 3-dc cluster

1- ch 2.

2 and 3- [yo and insert hook into the same ch-1 space, yo and pull up a loop, yo and draw through 2 loops on hook] twice. (3 loops on hook)

4- yo and draw through all 3 loops on the hook to complete the beg 3-dc cluster.

Round 19- 3-dc cluster

1- yo and insert hook into the ch-1 space indicated, yo and pull up a loop, yo and draw through 2 loops on hook. (2 loops on hook)

2 and 3- [yo and insert hook into the same space, yo and pull up a loop, draw through 2 loops on hook] twice. (4 loops on hook)

4- yo and draw through all 4 loops to complete the 3-dc cluster.

Round 19- 3-FPdc decrease(RS)

1- you will be working around the posts of the 2 FPdc circled in the first photo.

2- keeping the last loop of each FPdc on the hook, FPdc twice around the first FPdc. (3 loops on hook).

3- FPdc around the second FPdc. (4 loops on hook).

4- yo and draw through all 4 loops on the hook to complete the 3-FPdc decrease.

Round 19- 3-FPdc decrease(LS)

1- you will be working around the posts of the 2 FPdc circled in the first photo.

2- keeping the last loop of each FPdc on the hook, FPdc around the first FPdc. (2 loops on hook).

3- FPdc twice around the next FPdc. (4 loops on hook).

4- yo and draw through all 4 loops on the hook to complete the 3-FPdc decrease.

Round 20

ch 3 (counts as first dc), [3 dc in next ch-3 space, dc in next 3-dc cluster] twice, sc in next ch-3 space, ch 3, sc in next ch-3 space, ch 5, sc in next ch-3 space, ch 3, sc in next ch-3 space, dc in next 3-dc cluster, [3 dc in next ch-3 space, dc in next 3-dc cluster] twice, ch 3, skip next ch-3 space, sc in next ch-3 space, ch 3, skip next ch-3 space, dc in next 3-dc cluster, [3 dc in next ch-3 space, dc in next 3-dc cluster] twice, sc in next ch-3 space, ch 3, sc in next ch-3 space, ch 5, sc in next ch-3 space, ch 3, sc in next ch-3 space, dc in next 3-dc cluster, [3 dc in next ch-3 space, dc in next 3-dc cluster] twice, ch 3, skip next ch-3 space, sc in next ch-3 space, ch 3, skip next ch-3 space, repeat from around, slip st to third ch of first dc.

(144 dc, 40 sc, 32 ch-3 spaces, 8 ch-5 spaces)

Round 21

ch 1, BPdc around same st, [ch 1, BPdc around next dc] 8 times, sc in next ch-3 space, dc in next ch-5 space, [ch 1, dc] 6 times in same ch-5 space, sc in next ch-3 space, BPdc around next dc, [ch 1, BPdc around next dc] 8 times, skip next 2 ch-3 spaces,   BPdc around next dc, [ch 1, BPdc around next dc] 8 times, sc in next ch-3 space, dc in next ch-5 space, [ch 1, dc] 6 times in same ch-5 space, sc in next ch-3 space, BPdc around next dc, [ch 1, BPdc around next dc] 8 times, skip next 2 ch-3 spaces, repeat from   around, slip st to first BPdc.

(144 BPdc, 176 ch-1 spaces, 16 sc, 56 dc)

Round 22

slip st into next ch-1 space and in next BPdc, ch 1, 2-FPdc cluster around same st, [ch 1, 2-FPdc cluster around next BPdc] 7 times, skip next sc and next dc, sc in next ch-1 space, [sc in next dc, sc in next ch-1 space] twice, [sc, ch 2, sc] in next dc, sc in next ch-1 space, [sc in next dc, sc in next ch-1 space] twice, skip next dc and next sc, 2-FPdc cluster around next BPdc, [ch 1, 2-FPdc cluster around next BPdc] 7 times, skip next ch-1 space, sc in between next 2 BPdc, skip next BPdc, 2-FPdc cluster around next BPdc, [ch 1, 2-FPdc cluster around next BPdc] 7 times, skip next sc and next dc, sc in next ch-1 space, [sc in next dc, sc in next ch-1 space] twice, [sc, ch 2, sc] in next dc, sc in next ch-1 space, [sc in next dc, sc in next ch-1 space] twice, skip next dc and next sc, 2-FPdc cluster around next BPdc, [ch 1, 2-FPdc cluster around next BPdc] 7 times, skip next ch-1 space, sc in between next 2 BPdc, skip next BPdc, repeat from   around, slip st to first 2-FPdc cluster, fasten off color 1.

(128 2-FPdc clusters, 112 ch-1 spaces, 104 sc, 8 ch-2 spaces)

Round 22- 2-FPdc cluster

1- yo and insert hook from front to back around the post of the BPdc indicated.

2- yo and pull up a loop.

3- yo and draw through 2 loops on hook. (2 loops on hook).

4- yo and insert hook from front to back around the same st, yo and pull up a loop, yo and draw through 2 loops on hook. (3 loops on

hook)

5- yo and draw through all 3 loops on hook to complete the 2-FPdc cluster.

Round 22- sc in between next 2 BPdc

sc in the space between the next 2 BPdc circled in the first photo.

Round 23

join color 2 in next ch-1 space, ch 1, sc in same space, [picot, sc in next ch-1 space] 6 times, sc-BLO in each of next 3 sc, picot, sc-BLO in each of next 2 sc, picot, sc-BLO in next sc, sc-BLO in first ch of next ch-2 space, large picot, sc-BLO in second ch of same ch-2 space, sc-BLO in next sc, picot, sc-BLO in each of next 2 sc, picot, sc-BLO in each of next 3 sc, sc in next ch-1 space, [picot, sc in next ch-1 space] 6 times, ch 1, slip st in next sc, ch 1,   sc in next ch-1 space, [picot, sc in next ch-1 space] 6 times, sc-BLO in each of next 3 sc, picot, sc-BLO in each of next 2 sc, picot, sc-BLO in next sc, sc-BLO in first ch of next ch-2 space, large picot, sc-BLO in second ch of same ch-2 space, sc-BLO in next sc, picot, sc-BLO in each of next 2 sc, picot, sc-BLO in each of next 3 sc, sc in next ch-1 space, [picot, sc in next ch-1 space] 6 times, ch 1, slip st in next sc, ch 1, repeat from   around, slip st to first sc, fasten off and weave in ends.

(112 sc, 128 picots, 112 sc-BLO, 8 large picots, 16 ch-1 spaces, 8 slip sts)

Blocking and Finishing

It is optional but recommended to block your finished piece. Fill a bowl with water and add some liquid starch if you prefer the doily to be lightly stiffened. Soak and gently press out any excess liquid, being careful not to pull or twist on the stitches. Lay it flat on a blocking mat and pin the doily working from the center out to the edges. Allow to dry completely before removing the pins.

Sweetheart Soiree

Materials

size 10 thread in 2 colors-

color 1- 125-150 yards

color 2- 5-10 yards

1.75 mm hook

yarn needle

scissors

Stitch Abbreviations

beg- beginning

BPdc- back post double crochet

ch(s)- chains

dc- double crochet

FPdc- front post double crochet

FPsc- front post single crochet

hdc- half double crochet

sc- single crochet

sc-BLO- single crochet back loop only

st(s)- stitch(es)

yo- yarn over

Special Stitches

beg 4-dc cluster- (uses same ch-3 space and next ch-3 space), ch 2, keeping last loop of each dc on hook, dc in same space, 2 dc in next ch-3 space, yo and draw through all 4 loops on hook.

4-dc cluster- (uses same ch-3 space and next ch-3 space), keeping last loop of each dc on hook, 2 dc in same ch-3 space, 2 dc in next ch-3 space, yo and draw through all 5 loops on hook.

2-dc decrease- keeping last loop of each dc on hook, dc in each of the next 2 sts indicated, yo and draw through all 3 loops on hook.

3-dc decrease- keeping last loop of each dc on hook, dc in each of the next 3 sts indicated, yo and draw through all 4 loops on hook.

2-FPdc decrease- keeping last loop of each dc on hook, FPdc around the post each of the next 2 sts indicated, yo and draw through all 3 loops on hook.

beg 3-dc cluster- ch 2, keeping last loop of each dc on hook, 2 dc in the same ch-3 space indicated, yo and draw through all 3 loops on hook.

3-dc cluster- keeping last loop of each dc on hook, 3 dc in the ch-3 space indicated, yo and draw through all 4 loops on hook.

4-FPdc decrease- keeping last loop of each FPdc on hook, FPdc around the post of each of the next 4 sts indicated, yo and draw through all 5 loops on hook.

special FPdc decrease- (uses the next 4 FP sts), 2-FPdc decrease around the post of next 2 sts indicated, [2-FPdc decrease around the post of same st as second leg of last 2-FPdc decrease made and next st indicated] twice.

3-FPdc decrease- keeping last loop of each FPdc on hook, FPdc around the post of each of the next 3 sts indicated, yo and draw through all 4 loops on hook.

2-FPdc cluster- keeping last loop of each FPdc on hook, FPdc twice around the post of the BPdc indicated, yo and draw through all 3 loops on hook.

picot- ch 3, slip st in third ch from hook.

large picot- ch 5, slip st in fifth ch from hook.

Notes

[ ] - work enclosed instructions the amount of times indicated, or work enclosed instructions in the stitch or space indicated.

- repeat the following instructions the amount of times indicated.

( ) - Enclose additional information and the number of stitches at the end of a round.

Text highlighted in this color means there are photos and additional information below.

Instructions

ch 4, slip st in first ch to make a ring.

Round 1

ch 3 (counts as first dc), 15 dc in ring, slip st to third ch of first dc.

(16 dc)

Round 2

ch 1, sc in same st, [ch 3, skip next dc, sc in next dc] 7 times, ch 1, hdc in first sc to make last ch-3 space.

(8 sc, 8 ch-3 spaces)

Round 3

beg 4-dc cluster using same ch-3 space and next ch-3 space,

Repeat from   to   around-

ch 5, 4-dc cluster using same ch-3 space and next ch-3 space

ch 2, dc in beg 4-dc cluster to make last ch-5 space.

(8 4-dc clusters, 8 ch-5 spaces)

Beg 4-dc cluster

1- You'll be working in the 2 ch-3 spaces circled.

2- ch 2.

3- yo and insert hook into the same ch-3 space and pull up a loop, yo and draw through 2 loops on hook. (2 loops on hook)

4- yo and insert hook into the next ch-3 space, yo and pull up a loop, yo and draw through 2 loops on hook. (3 loops on hook)

5- yo and insert hook into the same ch-3 space, yo and pull up a loop, yo and draw through 2 loops on hook. (4 loops on hook)

6- yo and draw through all 4 loops on hook to complete the beg 4-dc cluster.

4-dc cluster

1- You'll be working in the same ch-3 space and next ch-3 space, both circled in the first photo.

2- [yo and insert hook into the same ch-3 space, yo and pull up a loop, yo and draw through 2 loops on hook] twice. (3 loops on hook)

3- [yo and insert hook into the next ch-3 space, yo and pull up a loop, yo and draw through 2 loops on hook] twice. (5 loops on hook).

4- yo and draw through all 5 loops on hook to complete the 4-dc cluster.

Round 4

ch 1, 3 sc in same space, ch 3, slip st in third ch from hook (picot made),

Repeat from   to   around-

  [3 sc, ch 3, 3 sc] in next ch-5 space, picot

3 sc in same ch-5 space as first sc, ch 1, hdc in first sc to make last ch-3 space.

(48 sc, 8 ch-3 spaces)

Round 5

ch 8 (counts as first dc and ch-5 space), skip next 6 sc,

Repeat from to around-

[dc, ch 3, dc] in next ch-3 space, ch 5, skip next 6 sc

dc in same ch-3 space as first dc, ch 3, slip st to third ch of first dc.

(16 dc, 8 ch-3 spaces, 8 ch-5 spaces)

Round 6

ch 3 (counts as first dc), dc in same st, ch 3, sc in next ch-5 space, ch 3, 2 dc in next dc, ch 3,

skip next ch-3 space,

Repeat from to around-

2 dc in next dc, ch 3, sc in next ch-5 space, ch 3, 2 dc in next dc, ch 3, skip next ch-3 space

slip st to third ch of first dc.

(32 dc, 24 ch-3 spaces, 8 sc)

Round 7

ch 3 (counts as first dc), 2 dc in next dc, sc in next ch-3 space, ch 3, sc in next ch-3 space,

2 dc in next dc, dc in next dc, ch 5,

Repeat from   to   around-

  dc in next dc, 2 dc in next dc, sc in next ch-3 space, ch 3, sc in next ch-3 space, 2 dc in next dc,

dc in next dc, ch 5

slip st to third ch of first dc.

(48 dc, 8 ch-5 spaces, 16 sc, 8 ch-3 spaces)

Round 8

ch 2, dc in next dc (first 2-dc decrease made), 2 dc in next dc, sc in next ch-3 space, 2 dc in next dc,

2-dc decrease in next 2 dc, ch 3, [dc, ch 3] twice in center ch of next ch-5 space,

Repeat from   to   around-

  2-dc decrease in next 2 dc, 2 dc in next dc, sc in next ch-3 space, 2 dc in next dc,

2-dc decrease in next 2 dc, ch 3,[dc, ch 3] twice in center ch of next ch-5 space

slip st to top of first 2-dc decrease.

(48 dc, 16 2-dc decreases, 24 ch-3 spaces)

2-dc decrease in next 2 dc

1- yo and insert hook into the first dc indicated, yo and pull up a loop, yo and draw through 2 loops on hook. (2 loops on hook)

2- yo and insert hook into the second dc indicated, yo and pull up a loop, yo and draw through 2 loops on hook. (3 loops on hook)

3- yo and draw through all 3 loops on hook to complete the 2-dc decrease.

Round 9

ch 2, dc in next dc (first 2-dc decrease made), dc in each of next 3 sts, 2-dc decrease in next 2 sts, ch 3, skip next ch-3 space, 9 dc in next ch-3 space (mark 4th dc of 9 dc group just made for st placement on Round 11), ch 3, skip next ch-3 space,

Repeat from   to   around-

2-dc decrease in next 2 sts, dc in each of next 3 sts, 2-dc decrease in next 2 sts, ch 3,

skip next ch-3 space, 9 dc in next ch-3 space, ch 3, skip next ch-3 space slip st to top of first 2-dc decrease.

(96 dc, 16 2-dc decreases, 16 ch-3 spaces)

Round 10

ch 2, dc in next dc (first 2-dc decrease made), dc in next dc, 2-dc decrease in next 2 sts, ch 3,

dc in next dc, ch 1, [BPdc in next dc, ch 1] 7 times, dc in next dc, ch 3, skip next ch-3 space,

Repeat from   to   around-

2-dc decrease in next 2 sts, dc in next dc, 2-dc decrease in next 2 sts, ch 3, dc in next dc, ch 1,

[BPdc in next dc, ch 1] 7 times, dc in next dc, ch 3, skip next ch-3 space

slip st to top of first 2- dc decrease.

(16 2-dc decreases, 24 dc, 80 ch-1 spaces, 56 BPdc, 16 ch-3 spaces)

Round 11

ch 2, 2-dc decrease in next 2 sts (counts as first 3-dc decrease), ch 3, FPdc twice around next dc,

sc in next ch-1 space, [ch 1, sc in next ch-1 space] 3 times,

3-dc decrease in marked dc on Round 9 and next 2 dc on Round 9, sc in next ch-1 space on Round 10, [ch 1, sc in next ch-1 space] 3 times,

FPdc twice around next dc (optional- work second FPdc behind the first FPdc), ch 3,

skip next ch-3 space,

Repeat from to around-

3-dc decrease in next 3 sts, ch 3, FPdc twice around next dc, sc in next ch-1 space,

[ch 1, sc in next ch-1 space] 3 times,

3-dc decrease in the 4th, 5th, and 6th dcs of the next 9 dc group on Round 9 directly below, sc in next ch-1 space on Round 10, [ch 1, sc in next ch-1 space] 3 times,

FPdc twice around next dc (optional- work second FPdc behind the first FPdc), ch 3,

skip next ch-3 space

slip st to top of first 3-dc decrease.

(16 3-dc decreases, 16 ch-3 spaces, 32 FPdc, 64 sc, 56 ch-1 spaces)

First 3-dc decrease

1- ch 2.

2- [yo and insert hook into the next st indicated and pull up a loop, yo and draw through 2 loops on hook] twice. (3 loops on hook)

3- yo and draw through all 3 loops on hook to complete the first 3-dc decrease.

Patterns for Vintage Doilies

How to make a FPdc (front post double crochet)

1- yo.

2- insert hook from front to back around the post of the st indicated.

3 and 4- yo and pull up a loop, [yo and draw through 2 loops on hook] twice to complete the the FPdc.

3-dc decrease in marked dc on Round 9 and next 2 dc on Round 9

1- You'll be working in the 3 dcs underlined on Round 9, the marked dc and next 2 dc.

2- yo and insert hook in the first dc indicated.

3- yo and pull up a loop, yo and draw through 2 loops on hook. (2 loops on hook)

4- yo and insert hook in the second dc indicated, yo and pull up a loop, yo and draw through 2 loops on hook. (3 loops on hook)

5- yo and insert hook in the third dc indicated, yo and pull up a loop, yo and draw through 2 loops on hook. (4 loops on hook)

6- yo and draw through all 4 loops on hook to complete the 3-dc decrease.

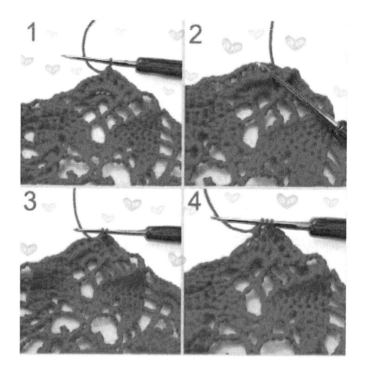

Optional- work second FPdc behind the first FPdc

1- After making the first FPdc, move it forward slightly so you can work behind it.

2- yo and insert hook from front to back around the same st.

3- yo and pull up a loop, [yo and draw through 2 loops on hook] twice.

Round 12

ch 6 (counts as first dc and ch-3 space), 2-FPdc decrease around next 2 FPdc, FPdc around same st,

[sc in next ch-1 space, ch 1] 3 times, FPsc around next 3-dc decrease,

[ch 1, sc in next ch-1 space] 3 times, FPdc around next FPdc,

2-FPdc decrease around same st and next FPdc

(optional- work first leg of 2-FPdc decrease behind the last FPdc made), ch 3,

Repeat from   to   around-

  dc in next 3-dc decrease, ch 3, 2-FPdc decrease around next 2 FPdc, FPdc around same st,

[sc in next ch-1 space, ch 1] 3 times, FPsc around next 3-dc decrease,

[ch 1, sc in next ch-1 space] 3 times, FPdc around next FPdc,

2-FPdc decrease around same st and next FPdc

(optional- work first leg of 2-FPdc decrease behind the last FPdc made), ch 3

slip st to third ch of first dc.

(8 dc, 16 ch-3 spaces, 16 2-FPdc decreases, 16 FPdc, 48 sc, 48 ch-1 spaces, 8 FPsc)

Round 13

ch 6 (counts as first dc and ch-3 space), dc in same st, ch 3, 2-FPdc decrease around next 2 FP sts,

FPdc around same st, sc in next ch-1 space, [ch 1, sc in next ch-1 space] 5 times,

FPdc around next FPdc, 2-FPdc decrease around same st and next st

(optional- work first leg of 2-FPdc decrease behind the last FPdc made), ch 3,

Repeat from   to   around-

[dc, ch 3] twice in next dc, 2-FPdc decrease around next 2 FP sts, FPdc around same st,

sc in next ch-1 space, [ch 1, sc in next ch-1 space] 5 times, FPdc around next FPdc,

2-FPdc decrease around same st and next st

(optional- work first leg of 2-FPdc decrease behind the last FPdc made), ch 3

slip st to third ch of first dc.

(16 dc, 24 ch-3 spaces, 16 2-FPdc decreases, 16 FPdc, 48 sc, 40 ch-1 spaces)

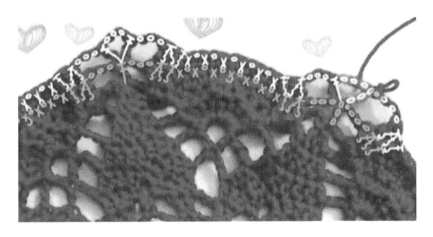

Round 14

ch 5 (counts as first dc and ch-2 space), 3 dc in center ch of next ch-3 space, ch 2, dc in next dc, ch 3,

2-FPdc decrease around next 2 FP sts, FPdc around same st, sc in next ch-1 space,

[ch 1, sc in next ch-1 space] 4 times, FPdc around next FPdc,

2-FPdc decrease around same st and next st

(optional- work first leg of 2-FPdc decrease behind the last FPdc made), ch 3,

Repeat from to around-

  dc in next dc, ch 2, 3 dc in center ch of next ch-3 space, ch 2, dc in next dc, ch 3,

2-FPdc decrease around next 2 FP sts, FPdc around same st, sc in next ch-1 space,

[ch 1, sc in next ch-1 space] 4 times, FPdc around next FPdc,

2-FPdc decrease around same st and next st

(optional- work first leg of 2-FPdc decrease behind the last FPdc made), ch 3

slip st to third ch of first dc.

(40 dc, 16 ch-2 spaces, 16 ch-3 spaces, 16 2-FPdc decreases, 16 FPdc, 40 sc, 32 ch-1 spaces)

Round 15

ch 6 (counts as first dc and ch-3 space), FPdc twice around next dc, FPdc around next dc,

FPdc twice around next dc (optional- work second FPdc behind the first FPdc), ch 3, dc in next dc,

ch 3, 2-FPdc decrease around next 2 FP sts, FPdc around same st, sc in next ch-1 space,

[ch 1, sc in next ch-1 space] 3 times, FPdc around next FPdc,

2-FPdc decrease around same st and next st

(optional- work first leg of 2-FPdc decrease behind the last FPdc made), ch 3,

dc in next dc, ch 3, FPdc twice around next dc, FPdc around next dc,

FPdc twice around next dc (optional- work second FPdc behind the first FPdc), ch 3, dc in next dc,

ch 3, 2-FPdc decrease around next 2 FP sts, FPdc around same st, sc in next ch-1 space,

[ch 1, sc in next ch-1 space] 3 times, FPdc around next FPdc,

2-FPdc decrease around same st and next st

(optional- work first leg of 2-FPdc decrease behind the last FPdc made), ch 3

slip st to third ch of first dc.

(16 dc, 32 ch-3 spaces, 56 FPdc, 16 2-FPdc decreases, 32 sc, 24 ch-1 spaces)

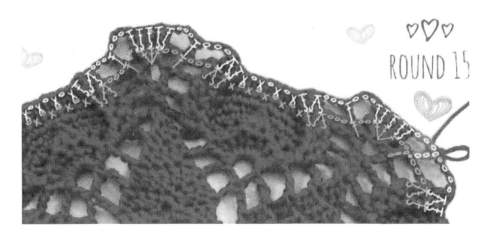

Round 16

ch 3 (counts as first dc), dc in same st, ch 3, FPdc twice around next FPdc,

FPdc around each of next 3 FPdc, FPdc twice around next FPdc

(optional- work second FPdc behind the first FPdc), ch 3, dc twice in next dc, ch 3,

2-FPdc decrease around next 2 FP sts, FPdc around same st, sc in next ch-1 space,

[ch 1, sc in next ch-1 space] twice, FPdc around next FPdc,

2-FPdc decrease around same st and next st

(optional- work first leg of the 2-FPdc decrease behind the last FPdc made), ch 3,

Repeat from to around-

  dc twice in next dc, ch 3, FPdc twice around next FPdc, FPdc around each of next 3 FPdc,

FPdc twice around next FPdc (optional- work second FPdc behind the first FPdc), ch 3,

dc twice in next dc, ch 3, 2-FPdc decrease around next 2 FP sts,

FPdc around same st, sc in next ch-1 space, [ch 1, sc in next ch-1 space] twice,

FPdc around next FPdc, 2-FPdc decrease around same st and next st

(optional- work first leg of the 2-FPdc decrease behind the last FPdc made), ch 3

slip st to third ch of first dc.

(32 dc, 32 ch-3 spaces, 72 FPdc, 16 2-FPdc decreases, 24 sc, 16 ch-1 spaces)

Round 17

ch 3 (counts as first dc), dc in same st, dc twice in next dc, ch 3, FPdc twice around next FPdc,

FPdc around next FPdc, 2-FPdc decrease around next 2 FPdc, ch 3,

2-FPdc decrease around same st and next FPdc, FPdc around next FPdc,

FPdc twice around next FPdc (optional- work second FPdc behind the first FPdc), ch 3,

dc twice in each of next 2 dc, ch 3, 2-FPdc decrease around next 2 FP sts, FPdc around same st,

sc in next ch-1 space, ch 1, sc in next ch-1 space, FPdc around next FPdc,

2-FPdc decrease around same st and next st

(optional- work first leg of 2-FPdc decrease behind the last FPdc made), ch 3,

Repeat from   to   around-

dc twice in each of next 2 dc, ch 3, FPdc twice around next FPdc, FPdc around next FPdc,

2-FPdc decrease around next 2 FPdc, ch 3, 2-FPdc decrease around same st and next FPdc,

FPdc around next FPdc, FPdc twice around next FPdc

(optional- work second FPdc behind the first FPdc), ch 3, dc twice in each of next 2 dc, ch 3,

2-FPdc decrease around next 2 FP sts, FPdc around same st, sc in next ch-1 space, ch 1,

sc in next ch-1 space, FPdc around next FPdc, 2-FPdc decrease around same st and next st

(optional- work first leg of 2-FPdc decrease behind the last FPdc made), ch 3

slip st to third ch of first dc.

(64 dc, 40 ch-3 spaces, 64 FPdc, 32 2-FPdc decreases, 16 sc, 8 ch-1 spaces)

Round 18

ch 4 (counts as first dc and ch-1 space), dc in next dc, [ch 1, dc in next dc] twice, ch 3,

FPdc twice around next FPdc, FPdc around next FPdc, 2-FPdc decrease around next 2 FP sts, ch 3,

sc in next ch-3 space, ch 3, 2-FPdc decrease around next 2 FP sts, FPdc around next FPdc,

FPdc twice around next FPdc (optional- work second FPdc behind the first FPdc), ch 3, dc in next dc, [ch 1, dc in next dc] 3 times, ch 3, 2-FPdc decrease around next 2 FP sts, FPdc around same st,

sc in next ch-1 space, FPdc around next FPdc, 2-FPdc decrease around same st and next st

(optional- work first leg of 2-FPdc decrease behind the last FPdc made), ch 3,

Repeat from   to   around-

dc in next dc, [ch 1, dc in next dc] 3 times, ch 3, FPdc twice around next FPdc,

FPdc around next FPdc, 2-FPdc decrease around next 2 FP sts, ch 3, sc in next ch-3 space, ch 3,

2-FPdc decrease around next 2 FP sts, FPdc around next FPdc, FPdc twice around next FPdc

(optional- work second FPdc behind the first FPdc), ch 3, dc in next dc, [ch 1, dc in next dc] 3 times,

ch 3, 2-FPdc decrease around next 2 FP sts, FPdc around same st, sc in next ch-1 space,

FPdc around next FPdc, 2-FPdc decrease around same st and next st

(optional- work first leg of 2-FPdc decrease behind the last FPdc made), ch 3

slip st to third ch of first dc.

(64 dc, 48 ch-1 spaces, 48 ch-3 spaces, 64 FPdc, 32 2-FPdc decreases, 8 sc)

Round 19

slip st in next ch-1 space, beg 3-dc cluster in same space, ch 3,

[3-dc cluster in next ch-1 space, ch 3] twice, 4-FPdc decrease around next 4 FP sts, ch 3,

3 dc in next sc, ch 3, 4-FPdc decrease around next 4 FP sts, ch 3, skip next ch-3 space,

[3-dc cluster in next ch-1 space, ch 3] 3 times, special FPdc decrease around next 4 FP sts, ch 3,

skip next ch-3 space,

Repeat from to around-

[3-dc cluster in next ch-1 space, ch 3] 3 times, 4-FPdc decrease around next 4 FP sts, ch 3,

3 dc in next sc, ch 3, 4-FPdc decrease around next 4 FP sts, ch 3, skip next ch-3 space,

[3-dc cluster in next ch-1 space, ch 3] 3 times, special FPdc decrease around next 4 FP sts, ch 3,

skip next ch-3 space

slip st to top of first 3-dc cluster.

(48 3-dc clusters, 80 ch-3 spaces, 16 4-FPdc decreases, 24 dc, 8 special FPdc decreases)

Beg 3-dc cluster

1- ch 2.

2 and 3- [yo and insert hook into the same ch-1 space, yo and pull up a loop, yo and draw through 2 loops on hook] twice. (3 loops on hook)

4- yo and draw through all 3 loops on the hook to complete the beg 3-dc cluster.

3-dc cluster

1- yo and insert hook into the ch-1 space indicated, yo and pull up a loop, yo and draw through 2 loops on hook. (2 loops on hook)

2 and 3- [yo and insert hook into the same space, yo and pull up a loop, draw through 2 loops on hook] twice. (4 loops on hook)

4- yo and draw through all 4 loops to complete the 3-dc cluster.

4-FPdc decrease around next 4 FP sts

1- You'll be working around the posts of the next 4 FP sts indicated.

2- yo and insert hook from front to back around the post of the first FP st, yo and pull up a loop, yo and draw through 2 loops on hook, [yo and insert hook from front to back around the the next FP st, yo and pull up a loop, yo and draw through 2 loops on hook] 3 times. (5 loops on hook)

3- yo and draw through all 5 loops on hook to complete the 4-FPdc decrease.

Special FPdc decrease around next 4 FP sts

1- You'll be working around the posts of the next 4 FP sts indicated.

2- 2-FPdc decrease around the first 2 FP sts.

3 and 4- 2-FPdc decrease around the post of same st as second leg of last 2-FPdc decrease made and next FPdc.

Round 20

ch 3 (counts as first dc), [3 dc in next ch-3 space, dc in next 3-dc cluster] twice, sc in next ch-3 space, ch 3, sc in next ch-3 space, dc in next dc, 3 dc in next dc, dc in next dc, sc in next ch-3 space, ch 3,

sc in next ch-3 space, dc in next 3-dc cluster, [3 dc in next ch-3 space, dc in next 3-dc cluster] twice,

ch 3, 3-FPdc decrease around next 3 FP sts, ch 3,

Repeat from   to   around-

   dc in next 3-dc cluster, [3 dc in next ch-3 space, dc in next 3-dc cluster] twice, sc in next ch-3 space, ch 3, sc in next ch-3 space, dc in next dc, 3 dc in next dc, dc in next dc, sc in next ch-3 space, ch 3,

sc in next ch-3 space, dc in next 3-dc cluster, [3 dc in next ch-3 space, dc in next 3-dc cluster] twice,

ch 3, 3-FPdc decrease around next 3 FP sts, ch 3

slip st to third ch of first dc.

(184 dc, 32 sc, 16 ch-3 spaces, 8 3-FPdc decreases)

3-FPdc decrease around next 3 FP sts

1- You'll be working around the posts of the next 3 FP sts of the special FPdc decrease.

2- yo and insert hook from front to back around the post of the first st indicated, yo and pull up a loop, yo and draw through 2 loops on hook. [yo and insert hook from front to back around the next st indicated, yo and pull up a loop, yo and draw through 2 loops on hook] twice. (4 loops on hook)

3- yo and draw through all 4 loops on hook to complete the 3-FPdc decrease.

Round 21

ch 1, BPdc around same st, [ch 1, BPdc around next dc] 8 times, sc in next ch-3 space,

[dc in next dc, ch 1] twice, [dc, ch 1] 3 times in next dc, dc in next dc, ch 1, dc in next dc,

sc in next ch-3 space, BPdc around next dc, [ch 1, BPdc around next dc] 8 times,

skip next 2 ch-3 spaces,

Repeat from   to   around-

  BPdc around next dc, [ch 1, BPdc around next dc] 8 times, sc in next ch-3 space,

[dc in next dc, ch 1] twice, [dc, ch 1] 3 times in next dc, dc in next dc, ch 1, dc in next dc,

sc in next ch-3 space, BPdc around next dc, [ch 1, BPdc around next dc] 8 times,

skip next 2 ch-3 spaces

slip st to first BPdc.

(144 BPdc, 176 ch-1 spaces, 16 sc, 56 dc)

Round 22

slip st into next ch-1 space and in next BPdc, ch 1, 2-FPdc cluster around same st,

[ch 1, 2-FPdc cluster around next BPdc] 7 times, skip next sc and next dc, sc in next ch-1 space,

[sc in next dc, sc in next ch-1 space] twice, [sc, ch 2, sc] in next dc, sc in next ch-1 space,

[sc in next dc, sc in next ch-1 space] twice, skip next dc and next sc, 2-FPdc cluster around next BPdc, [ch 1, 2-FPdc cluster around next BPdc] 7 times, skip next ch-1 space, sc in between next 2 BPdc,

skip next BPdc,

Repeat from   to   around-

2-FPdc cluster around next BPdc, [ch 1, 2-FPdc cluster around next BPdc] 7 times,

skip next sc and next dc, sc in next ch-1 space, [sc in next dc, sc in next ch-1 space] twice,

[sc, ch 2, sc] in next dc, sc in next ch-1 space, [sc in next dc, sc in next ch-1 space] twice, skip next dc and next sc, 2-FPdc cluster around next BPdc,

[ch 1, 2-FPdc cluster around next BPdc] 7 times, skip next ch-1 space, sc in between next 2 BPdc,

skip next BPdc

slip st to first 2-FPdc cluster, fasten off color 1.

(128 2-FPdc clusters, 112 ch-1 spaces, 104 sc, 8 ch-2 spaces)

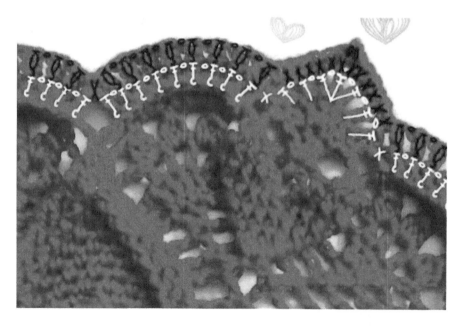

2-FPdc cluster

1- yo and insert hook from front to back around the post of the BPdc indicated.

2- yo and pull up a loop.

3- yo and draw through 2 loops on hook. (2 loops on hook)

4- yo and insert hook from front to back around the same st, yo and pull up a loop, yo and draw through 2 loops on hook. (3 loops on hook)

5- yo and draw through all 3 loops on hook to complete the 2-FPdc cluster.

sc in between next 2 BPdc

Round 23

join color 2 in next ch-1 space, ch 1, sc in same space, [picot, sc in next ch-1 space] 6 times,

sc-BLO (back loop only) in each of next 3 sc, picot, sc-BLO in each of next 2 sc, picot,

sc-BLO in next sc, sc-BLO in first ch of next ch-2 space, large picot, sc-BLO in second ch of same ch-2 space, sc-BLO in next sc, picot, sc-BLO in each of next 2 sc, picot, sc-BLO in each of next 3 sc, sc in next ch-1 space, [picot, sc in next ch-1 space] 6 times, ch 1,

slip st in next sc, ch 1,

Repeat from   to   around-

sc in next ch-1 space, [picot, sc in next ch-1 space] 6 times, sc-BLO in each of next 3 sc, picot,

sc-BLO in each of next 2 sc, picot, sc-BLO in next sc, sc-BLO in first ch of next ch-2 space,

large picot, sc-BLO in second ch of same ch-2 space, sc-BLO in next sc, picot,

sc-BLO in each of next 2 sc, picot, sc-BLO in each of next 3 sc, sc in next ch-1 space,

[picot, sc in next ch-1 space] 6 times, ch 1, slip st in next sc, ch 1

slip st to first sc, fasten off and weave in ends.

(112 sc, 128 picots, 112 sc-BLO, 8 large picots, 16 ch-1 spaces, 8 slip sts)

Join color 2 in next ch-1 space

Blocking and Finishing

It is optional but recommended to block your finished piece. Fill a bowl with water and add some liquid starch if you prefer the doily to be lightly stiffened. Soak and gently press out any excess liquid, being careful not to pull or twist on the stitches. Lay it flat on a blocking mat and pin the doily working from the center out to the edges. Allow to dry completely before removing the pins.

Triple Flavor

Yarn: Schachenmayr Catania Trend (sport weight)

Color A 290 Pale Green approx 50 m/55 yd

Color B 291 Neo Mint approx 75 m/82 yd

Color C 292 Green Juice approx 75 m/82 yd

Hook: 3.0 mm

Measurements: ⬜ approx 37 cm / 14.5 in after blocking

Abbreviations (US terms)

st stitch

sl st slip stitch

ch chain

ch sp chain space

sc single crochet

dc double crochet

2dccl 2 double crochet cluster

dc2tog double crochet 2 together

picot ch 3, sl st in the first ch

* - * repeat around

{ - } repeat the indicated number of times

[-] work in the same st

Notes

Patterns for Vintage Doilies

• The first st on each round is replaced by:

sc ch 1

dc ch 3

or is worked as a standing st

• Close each round with a sl st to the first st, or an invisible join

• Stitch count in (-) at the end of each round

• Your work may become slightly wobbly, but will be flat after blocking

• Block your finished piece for best results

Color A

Round 1: ch 5, sl st in the first ch to form a ring, 16 dc in the ring (16 dc)

Round 2: *[2dccl, ch 2, 2dccl] in the same st, skip 1 st* (16 2dccl, 8 ch sp)

Round 3: sl st into ch sp, *3 sc in ch sp, skip 2dccl, 2 sc in the space between 2dccl, skip 2dccl* (40 sc)

Round 4: sl st in the next st (= the 2nd sc of 3), *[{1 dc, ch 1} 3 times, 1 dc] in the same st, skip 1 st, 1 dc in each of the next 2 st, skip 1 st* (48 dc, 24 ch sp)

Round 5: sl st into the 2nd ch sp, *7 dc in ch sp, ch 1, skip dc+ch sp+2 dc, 1 sc in the space between the 2 dc, ch 1, skip 2 dc+ch sp+dc* (56 dc, 16 ch-1 sp, 8 sc)

Round 6: 3 dc, [1 dc, ch 1, 1 dc] in the next st, 3 dc, dc2tog over the 2 ch-1 sp* (64 dc, 8 ch sp, 8xdc2tog)

Color B

Round 7: Start in any ch sp, *1 sc in ch sp, ch 6, skip 4 dc, 1 sc in the next st, ch 6, skip 4 dc* (16 sc, 16 ch sp)

Round 8: *[2dccl, ch 2, 2dccl] in sc, ch 3, 1 sc in ch sp, ch 3, 1 sc in the next ch sp, ch 3* (16 2dccl, 16 ch-2 sp, 24 ch-3 sp, 16 sc)

Round 9: sl st into ch sp, *[1 sc, ch 2, 1 sc] in ch-2 sp, skip 2dccl, {4 sc in the next ch sp, 1 sc in sc} 2 times, 4 sc in the next ch sp, skip 2dccl* (128 sc, 8 ch sp)

Round 10: sl st into ch sp, *7 dc in ch sp, skip 2 st, 1 sc, skip 2 st, 2 dc in the next st, 1 dc in each of the next 4 st, 2 dc in the next st, skip 2 st, 1 sc, skip 2 st* (120 dc, 16 sc)

Round 11: * {1 dc, ch 1} 3 times, [1 dc, ch 1, 1 dc] in the next st, {ch 1, 1 dc} 3 times, skip 2 st, 1 sc, skip 1 st, [1 dc, ch 1, 1 dc] in the next st, ch 1, [1 dc, ch 1, 1 dc] in the next st, skip 1 st, 1 sc, skip 2 st* (8x8 dc+7 ch sp, 8x4 dc+ch 3 sp, 16 sc)

Round 12: * {1 dc in dc, ch 1} 4 times, [1 dc, ch 1, 1 dc] in ch sp (= the 4th ch sp of 7), {ch 1, 1 dc in dc} 4 times, skip sc+dc+ch sp+dc, [1 dc, ch 1, 1 dc, ch 1, 1 dc] in ch sp (= the 2nd ch sp of 3), skip dc+ch sp+dc+sc* (8x10 dc+9 ch sp, 8x3 dc+ch 2 sp)

Round 13: * {1 dc in dc, 1 dc in ch sp} 4 times, 1 dc in dc, 3 dc in ch sp, {1 dc in dc, 1 dc in ch sp} 4 times, 1 dc in dc, skip 1 dc, 1 dc in ch sp, 1 dc in dc, 1 dc in ch

sp, skip 1 dc* (192 dc)

Color C

Round 14: Start in the 2nd dc of 3 worked in a ch sp, *[2dccl, ch 2, 2dccl] in the same st, ch 5, skip 5 st, 1 sc in the next st, ch 5 , skip 5 st, [2dccl, ch 2, 2dccl] in the next st, ch 5 , skip 5 st, 1 sc in the next st, ch 5, skip 5 st* (32 2dccl, 16 ch-2 sp, 32 ch-5 sp, 16 sc)

Round 15: sl st into ch sp, *7 dc in ch-2 sp, skip 2dccl, 1 sc in ch-5 sp right after the 2dccl, ch 6, skip sc, 1 sc in the next ch-5 sp right before the 2dccl, skip 2dccl* (112 dc, 16 ch sp, 32 sc)

Round 16: *3 dc, [1 dc, ch 1, 1 dc] in the next st, 4 dc, 3 dc in the center of ch sp, 1 dc in the next st* (178 dc, 16 ch sp)

Round 17: * {1 dc in dc, ch 1} 4 times, 1 dc in ch sp, {ch 1, 1 dc in dc} 5 times, skip 1 dc, 1 sc in the next dc, skip 1 dc, 1 dc in the next dc, ch 1* (16x11 dc+10 ch sp, 16 sc)

Round 18: sl st into ch sp, *{1 sc in ch sp, ch 1, skip dc} 3 times, 1 sc in ch sp, picot, skip dc, {1 sc in ch sp, ch 1, skip dc} 4 times, 1 sc in ch sp, skip dc, sl st in sc, skip dc, 1 sc in ch sp, ch 1, skip dc* (160 sc, 128 ch sp, 16 picot, 16 sl st)

Fasten off. Weave in all ends. Block your work

Starlight

Materials

size 10 crochet thread- 100 yards

1.75 mm hook

yarn needle

scissors

Stitch Abbreviations

ch- chain

hdc- half double crochet

dc- double crochet

sc- single crochet

st(s)- stitch(es)

yo- yarn over

Special Stitches

3-dc cluster- keeping last loop of each dc on hook, 3 dc in space indicated, yo and draw through all 4 loops on hook.

2-dc decrease- keeping last loop of each dc on hook, dc in each of next 2 dc, yo and draw through all 3 loops on hook.

5-dc decrease- keeping last loop of each dc on hook, dc in each of next 5 dc, yo and draw through all 6 loops on hook.

2-dc cluster- keeping last loop of each dc on hook, 2 dc in space indicated, yo and draw through all 3 loops on hook.

picot- ch 4, slip st in last 2-dc cluster made.

Notes

[] , { } - work enclosed instructions the amount of times indicated, or work enclosed instructions in the stitch or space indicated.

★ - repeat the following instructions the amount of times indicated.

() - Enclose additional information and the number of stitches at the end of a round.

Instructions

ch 6, slip st in 6th ch from hook to make a ring.

Round 1- ch 1, 12 sc in ring, slip st to first sc.

(12 sc)

Round 2- ch 1, sc in same st, [ch 2, sc in next sc] around, hdc in first sc to make last ch-2 space.

(12 sc, 12 ch-2 spaces)

Round 3- ch 1, sc in same space, ch 3, 3-dc cluster in next ch-2 space, [ch 3, sc in next ch-2 space, ch 3, 3-dc cluster in next ch-2 space] around, ch 1, hdc in first sc to make last ch-3 space.

(6 sc, 12 ch-3 spaces, 6 3-dc clusters)

Round 4- ch 1, sc in same space, [ch 4, sc in next ch-3 space] around, ch 1, dc in first sc to make last ch-3 space.

(12 sc, 12 ch-4 spaces)

Round 5- ch 1, sc in same space, ch 3, [3-dc cluster, ch 3, 3-dc cluster] in next ch-4 space, ★ ch 3, sc in next ch-4 space, ch 3, [3-dc cluster, ch 3, 3-dc cluster] in next ch-4 space, repeat from ★ around, ch 1, hdc in first sc to make last ch-3 space.

(6 sc, 18 ch-3 spaces, 12 3-dc clusters)

Round 6- ch 1, sc in same space, ch 5, [sc in next ch-3 space, ch 5] around, slip st to first sc.

(18 sc, 18 ch-5 spaces)

Round 7- slip st into center ch of next ch-5 space, ch 4 (counts as first dc and ch-1 space now and throughout), dc in same st, ch 3, sc in next ch-5 space, ch 5, sc in next ch-5 space, ch 3, ★ in center ch of next ch-5 space work- [dc, ch 1, dc, ch 1, dc], ch 3, sc in next ch-5 space, ch 5, sc in next ch-5 space, ch 3, repeat from ★ around, dc in same st as first dc, ch 1, slip st to third ch of first dc.

(18 dc, 12 ch-1 spaces, 12 ch-3 spaces, 6 ch-5 spaces)

Round 8- ch 5 (counts as first dc and ch-2 space now and throughout), 2 dc in next dc, ch 5, skip next ch-3 space, sc in next ch-5 space, ch 5, 2 dc in next dc, ch 2, ★ dc in next dc, ch 2, 2 dc in next dc, ch 5, skip next ch-3 space, sc in next ch-5 space, ch 5, 2 dc in next dc, ch 2, repeat from ★ around, slip st to third ch of first dc.

(30 dc, 12 ch-2 spaces, 12 ch-5 spaces, 6 sc)

Round 9- ch 4, dc in same st, ch 2, dc in next dc, 2 dc in next dc, sc in next ch-5 space, ch 5, sc in next ch-5 space, 2 dc in next dc, dc in next dc, ch 2, ★ in next dc work- [dc, ch 1, dc, ch 1, dc], ch 2, dc in next dc, 2 dc in next dc, sc in next ch-5 space, ch 5, sc in next ch-5 space, 2 dc in next dc, dc in next dc, ch 2, repeat from ★ around, dc in same st as first dc, ch 1, slip st to third ch of first dc.

(54 dc, 12 ch-1 spaces, 12 ch-2 spaces, 12 sc, 6 ch-5 spaces)

Round 10- ch 5, 2 dc in next dc, ch 3, dc in each of next 2 dc, 2 dc in next dc, sc in next ch-5 space, 2 dc in next dc, dc in each of next 2 dc, ch 3, 2 dc in next dc, ch 2, ★ dc in next dc, ch 2, 2 dc in next dc, ch 3, dc in each of next 2 dc, 2 dc in next dc, sc in next ch-5 space, 2 dc in next dc, dc in each of next 2 dc, ch 3, 2 dc in next dc, ch 2 repeat from ★ around, slip st to third ch of first dc.

(78 dc, 12 ch-2 spaces, 12 ch-3 spaces, 6 sc)

Round 11- ch 4, [dc, ch 1, dc] in same st, ch 2, dc in next dc, 2 dc in next dc, ch 3, 2-dc decrease in next 2 dc, dc in each of next 5 sts, 2-dc decrease in next 2 dc, ch 3, 2 dc in next dc, dc in next dc, ch 2, ★ in next dc work- [dc, ch 1, dc, ch 1, dc], ch 2, dc in next dc, 2 dc in next dc, ch 3, 2-dc decrease in next 2 dc, dc in each of next 5 sts, 2-dc decrease in next 2 dc, ch 3, 2 dc in next dc, dc in next dc, ch 2, repeat from ★ around, slip st to third ch of first dc.

(84 dc, 12 ch-1 spaces, 12 ch-2 spaces, 12 ch-3 spaces, 12 2-dc decreases)

Round 12- ch 3 (counts as first dc now and throughout), dc in same st, ch 2, dc in next dc, ch 2, 2 dc in next dc, ch 2, dc in each of next 3 dc, ch 3, skip next ch-3 space, 2-dc decrease in next 2 sts, dc in each of next 3 dc, 2-dc decrease in next 2 sts, ch 3, dc in each of next 3 dc, ch 2, ★ 2 dc in next dc, ch 2, dc in next dc, ch 2, 2 dc in next dc, ch 2, dc in each of next 3 dc, ch 3, skip next ch-3 space, 2-dc decrease in next 2 sts, dc in each of next 3 dc, 2-dc decrease in next 2 sts, ch 3, dc in each of next 3 dc, ch 2, repeat from ★ around, slip st to third ch of first dc.

(84 dc, 24 ch-2 spaces, 12 ch-3 spaces, 12 2-dc decreases)

Round 13- ch 3, dc in next dc, ch 2, dc in next dc, in same st work- [ch 1, dc] 4 times, ch 2, dc in each of next 2 dc, ch 3, dc in each of next 2 dc, 2 dc in next dc, ch 3, skip next ch-3 space, 5-dc decrease in next 5 sts, ch 3, 2 dc in next dc, dc in each of next 2 dc, ch 3, ★ dc in each of next 2 dc, ch 2, dc in next dc, in same st work- [ch 1, dc] 4 times, ch 2, dc in each of next 2 dc, ch 3, dc in each of next 2 dc, 2 dc in next dc, ch 3, skip next ch-3 space, 5-dc decrease in next 5 sts, ch 3, 2 dc in next dc, dc in each of next 2 dc, ch 3, repeat from ★ around, slip st to third ch of first dc.

(102 dc, 24 ch-3 spaces, 12 ch-2 spaces, 24 ch-1 spaces, 6 5-dc decreases)

Round 14- ch 3, dc in next dc, [ch 2, dc in next dc] 5 times, ch 2, dc in each of next 2 dc, ch 3, dc in each of next 4 dc, sc in next ch-3 space, ch 5, sc next ch-3 space, dc in each of next 4 dc, ch 3, ★ dc in each of next 2 dc, ch 2, [dc in next dc, ch 2] 5 times, dc in each of next 2 dc, ch 3, dc in each of next 4 dc, sc in next ch-3 space, ch 5, sc in next ch-3 space, dc in each of next 4 dc, ch 3, repeat from ★ around, slip st to third ch of first dc.

(102 dc, 36 ch-2 spaces, 12 ch-3 spaces, 12 sc, 6 ch-5 spaces)

Round 15- ch 3, dc in next dc, ch 2, [2 dc in next dc, ch 2] 5 times, dc in each of next 2 dc, ch 3, dc in each of next 4 dc, sc in next ch-5 space, dc in each of next 4 dc, ch 3, ★ dc in each of next 2 dc, ch 2, [2 dc in next dc, ch 2] 5 times, dc in each of next 2 dc, ch 3, dc in each of next 4 dc, sc in next ch-5 space, dc in each of next 4 dc, ch 3, repeat from ★ around, slip st to third ch of first dc.

(132 dc, 36 ch-2 spaces, 12 ch-3 spaces, 6 sc)

Round 16- ch 3, dc in next dc, ch 3, [dc in each of next 2 dc, ch 3] 6 times, 2-dc decrease in next 2 dc, dc in each of next 5 sts, 2-dc decrease in next 2 dc,a ch 3, ★ [dc in each of next 2 dc, ch 3] 7 times, 2-dc decrease in next 2 dc, dc in each of next 5 sts, 2-dc decrease in next 2 dc, ch 3, repeat from ★ around, slip st to third ch of first dc.

(114 dc, 48 ch-3 spaces, 12 2-dc decreases)

Picot Border

Round 17A- ch 3, dc in next dc, ch 4, [dc in each of next 2 dc, ch 4] 6 times, skip next ch-3 space, 2-dc decrease in next 2 sts, dc in each of next 3 dc, 2-dc decrease in next 2 sts, ch 4, ★ [dc in each of next 2 dc, ch 4] 7 times, skip next ch-3 space, 2-dc decrease in next 2 sts, dc in each of next 3 dc, 2-dc decrease in next 2 sts, ch 4, repeat from ★ around, slip st to third ch of first dc.

(102 dc, 48 ch-4 spaces, 12 2-dc decreases)

Round 18A- ch 2, dc in next dc (first 2-dc decrease made), ch 3, sc in next ch-4 space, ch 3, [2-dc decrease in next 2 dc, ch 3, sc in next ch-4 space, ch 3] 6 times, 5-dc decrease in next 5 sts, ch 3, sc in next ch-4 space, ch 3, ★ [2-dc decrease in next 2 dc, ch 3, sc in next ch-4 space, ch 3] 7 times, 5-dc decrease in next 5 sts, ch 3, sc in next ch-4 space, ch 3, repeat from ★ around, slip st to first 2-dc decrease.

(42 2-dc decreases, 96 ch-3 spaces, 48 sc, 6 5-dc decreases)

Round 19A- ch 1, sc in same st, ch 3, 2-dc cluster in next ch-3 space, picot, 2-dc cluster in next ch-3 space, ch 3, [sc in next 2-dc decrease, ch 3, 2-dc cluster in next ch-3 space, picot, 2-dc cluster in next ch-3 space, ch 3] 6 times, sc in next 5-dc decrease, ch 3, 2-dc cluster in next ch-3 space, picot, 2-dc cluster in next ch-3 space, ch 3, ★ [sc in next 2-dc decrease, ch 3, 2-dc cluster in next ch-3 space, picot, 2-dc cluster in next ch-3 space, ch 3] 7 times, sc in next 5-dc decrease, ch 3, 2-dc cluster in next ch-3 space, picot, 2-dc cluster in next ch-3 space, ch 3, repeat from ★ around, slip st to first sc, fasten off and weave in ends.

(48 sc, 96 ch-3 spaces, 96 2-dc clusters, 48 picots)

Alternate Border

Round 17B- ch 3, dc in next dc, [ch 4, dc in each of next 2 dc] 6 times, ch 3, skip next ch-3 space, 2-dc decrease in next 2 sts, dc in each of next 3 dc, 2-dc decrease in next 2 sts, ch 3, ★ dc in each of next 2 dc, [ch 4, dc in each of next 2 dc] 6 times, ch 3, skip next ch-3 space, 2-dc decrease in next 2 sts, dc in each of next 3 dc, 2-dc decrease in next 2 sts, ch 3, repeat from ★ around, slip st to third ch of first dc.

(102 dc, 36 ch-4 spaces, 12 ch-3 spaces, 12 2-dc decreases)

Round 18B- ch 2, dc in next dc (first 2-dc decrease made), [ch 3, sc in next ch-4 space, ch 3, 2-dc decrease in next 2 dc] 6 times, ch 3, skip next ch-3 space, 5-dc decrease in next 5 sts, ★ ch 3, 2-dc decrease in next 2 dc, [ch 3, sc in next ch-4 space, ch 3, 2-dc decrease in next 2 dc] 6 times, ch 3, skip next ch-3 space, 5-dc decrease in next 5 sts, repeat from ★ around, dc in first 2-dc decrease to make last ch-3 space.

(42 2-dc decreases, 84 ch-3 spaces, 36 sc, 6 5-dc decreases)

Round 19B- ch 1, [sc, ch 3, sc] in same space, {[sc, ch 3, sc] in next ch-3 space} 13 times, ch 3, ★ {[sc, ch 3, sc] in next ch-3 space} 14 times, ch 3, repeat from ★ around, slip st to first sc, fasten off and weave in ends.

(168 sc, 90 ch-3 spaces)

It is optional but recommended to block your finished piece. Fill a bowl with water and add some liquid starch if you prefer the doily to be lightly stiffened. Soak and gently press out any excess liquid, being careful not to pull or twist on the stitches. Lay it flat on a blocking mat and pin the doily working from the center out to the edges. Allow to dry completely before removing the pins.

Cherry Blossom Doily

Abbreviations:

ch = chain

sl st = slip stitch

dc = double crochet

beg = beginning

hdc = half double crochet

dc2tog = double crochet 2 together

dc3tog = double crochet 3 together

tr3tog = triple crochet 3 together

Special stitches:

ch3-picot = ch 3 and sl st in stitch below

v-stitch = dc+ch2+dc in same space

With color A ch 7, sl st in 1st ch to make a ring.

Round 1 = ch 4 (counts as 1st dc and 1 ch), (dc+ch1 in the ring) 14 times (15 dc), sl st in 3rd beg ch.

Round 2 = ch 5 (counts as 1st dc and 2 ch), (dc in next dc + ch2) 14 times (15 dc), sl st in 3rd beg ch.

Round 3 = ch 4 (counts as 1st dc and 1 ch), dc in next ch2-space + ch1, *dc in next dc + ch1, dc in next ch2-space + ch1, repeat from* (30 dc), sl st in 3rd beg ch.

Round 4 = ch 5 (counts as 1st dc and 2 ch), *dc in next dc + ch2, repeat from* (30 dc), sl st in 3rd beg ch.

Round 5 = repeat round 4.

Round 6 = ch 6 (counts as 1st dc and 3 ch), *dc in next dc + ch3, repeat from* (30 dc), sl st in 3rd beg ch, fasten off, cut off color A.

Round 7 = join color B in same stitch as last sl st and ch5 (counts as 1st dc and 2 ch), dc in same stitch, ch5, *skip next dc, in next dc make v-stitch = dc + ch2 + dc, ch5, repeat from* (15 v-stitches), sl st in 3rd beg ch.

Round 8 = ch 4 (counts as 1st hdc and 2 ch), hdc in next dc, ch2, *(hdc in next ch5-space + ch2) twice, (hdc in next dc + ch2) twice, repeat from* (60 hdc), sl st in 2nd beg ch.

Round 9 = ch 4 (counts as 1st hdc and 2 ch), *hdc in next hdc + ch2, repeat from* (60 hdc), sl st in 2nd beg ch, fasten off, cut off color B.

Round 10 = join color A in same stitch as last sl st and ch5 (counts as 1st dc and 2 ch), dc in same stitch, ch5, *skip next 2 hdc, in next hdc make v-stitch = dc + ch2 + dc, ch5, repeat from* (20 v-stitches), sl st in 3rd beg ch.

Round 11 = sl st in next ch2-space, ch5 (counts as 1st dc and 2 ch), dc in same space, ch2, v-stitch in 3rd ch of next ch5-space, ch2, *v-stitch in next ch2-space (v-stitch of last round), ch2, v-stitch in 3rd ch of next ch5-space, ch2, repeat from* (40 v-stitches), sl st in 3rd beg ch.

Round 12 = sl st in next ch2-space, ch5 (counts as 1st dc and 2 ch), dc in same space, ch2, *v-stitch in next ch2-space (v-stitch of last round), ch2, repeat from* (40 v-stitches), sl st in 3rd beg ch.

Round 13 = repeat round 12, fasten off, cut off color A.

Round 14 = join color B in ch2-space of v-stitch, ch2 and dc in same space (= beg dc2tog), ch6, *in next ch2-space of v-stitch dc2tog, ch6, repeat from*, sl st in top of beg dc2tog.

Round 15 = ch5 (counts as 1st hdc and 3 ch), hdc in next ch6-space, ch3, *hdc in next dc2tog, ch3, hdc in next ch6-space, ch3, repeat from*, sl st in 2nd beg ch.

Round 16 = ch5 (counts as 1st hdc and 3 ch), *hdc in next hdc, ch3, repeat from*, sl st in 2nd beg ch, fasten off, cut off color B.

Round 17 = join color A in first ch3-space, ch3 (counts as 1st dc), dc 3 in same space, ch5, skip next ch3-space and hdc, sc in next ch3-space, ch3, sc in next ch3-space, ch5, skip next hdc and ch3-space, *dc 4 in next ch3-space, ch5, skip next ch3-space and hdc, sc in next ch3-space, ch3, sc in next ch3-space, ch5, skip next hdc and ch3-space, repeat from*, sl st in 3rd beg ch.

Round 18 = ch3 (counts as 1st dc), dc 1 in each next 3 dc, ch5, sc in next ch5-space, ch4, sc in next ch3-space, ch4, sc in next ch5-space, ch5, *dc 1 in each next 4 dc, ch5, sc in next ch5-space, ch4, sc in next ch3-space, ch4, sc in next ch5-space, ch5, repeat from*, sl st in 3rd beg ch.

Round 19 = ch3 (counts as 1st dc), dc2tog in next 2 dc, dc 1 in next dc, ch7, skip next ch5-space, sc in next ch4-space, ch5, sc in next ch4-space, ch7, skip next ch5-space, *dc1 in next dc, dc2tog in next 2 dc, dc 1 in next dc, ch7, skip next ch5-space, sc in next ch4-space, ch5, sc in next ch4-space, ch7, skip next ch5-space, repeat from*, sl st in 3rd beg ch.

Round 20 = ch2 and dc2tog in next 2 stitches (= beg dc3tog), ch5, skip next ch7-space, in next ch5-space tr3tog + (ch4 + tr3tog) three times, ch5, skip next ch7-space, *dc3tog in next 3 stitches, ch5, skip next ch7-space, in next ch5-space tr3tog + (ch4 + tr3tog) three times, ch5, skip next ch7-space, repeat from*, sl st in top of beg dc3tog.

Round 21 = ch1, *sc in top of dc3tog, ch4, skip next ch5-space, dc3tog in next ch4-space, ch3-picot on top of dc3tog, (ch4, dc2tog with first leg going to the same space and second leg going to next ch4-space, ch4, dc3tog in same space where you did second leg of dc2tog, ch3-picot) twice, ch4, repeat from*, sl st in 1st sc.

Fasten off, cut off color A, weave in all ends and block the doily.

Made in the USA
Las Vegas, NV
11 May 2024

89787602R10075